Richard Edward White

The Cross of Monterey, and Other Poems

Richard Edward White

The Cross of Monterey, and Other Poems

ISBN/EAN: 9783337254322

Printed in Europe, USA, Canada, Australia, Japan

Cover: Foto ©Thomas Meinert / pixelio.de

More available books at **www.hansebooks.com**

THE

CROSS OF MONTEREY

AND OTHER POEMS

BY

RICHARD EDWARD WHITE.

SAN FRANCISCO:
THE CALIFORNIA PUBLISHING COMPANY,
No. 408 California Street.
1882.

CONTENTS.

BY THE CROSS OF MONTEREY.

Good Junipero the Padre,
    When 'twas dying of the day,
Sat beneath the dark tall pine-trees
    By the Cross of Monterey,
Listening as the simple red men
    Of their joys and sorrows told,
And their stories of the Missions,
    And their legends quaint and old.

And they told him when Portala
    Rested by the crescent bay,
Little dreaming he was gazing
    On the wished-for Monterey,
That this cross on shore he planted
    And the ground about it blessed,
And then he and his companions
    Journeyed northward on their quest.

And the Indians told the Padre
    That Portala's cross at night,
Gleaming with a wondrous splendor,
    Than the noon-sun was more bright,
And its mighty arms extended
    East and westward, O so far!
And its topmost point seemed resting
    Northward on the polar star.

And they told, when fear had vanished,
    How they gathered all around,
And their spears and arrows buried
    In the consecrated ground;
And they brought most fragrant blossoms,
    And rare ocean-shells in strings,
And they hung upon the cross-arms
    All their choicest offerings.

And the Padre told the Indians :
    "Ah, if rightly understood,
What you tell me of the cross here
    Has a meaning deep and good,

For that light is emblematic
That the time is near at hand
When the faith of Christ the Savior
Will illumine all the land.

"To the Cross cling, O my children!
In the storm and in the night,
When you wander, lost and weary,
It will be a guiding light;
Cling to it, and cares and sorrows
Very soon will all have passed,
And the palm and crown of glory
Will be given you at last."

Good Junipero the Padre
Thus unto the red men told
Of the emblem of salvation
And its story sweet and old,
Sitting by the crescent bay-side,
When 'twas dying of the day,
At the foot of dark tall pine-trees,
By the Cross of Monterey.

THE MIDNIGHT MASS.

Of the mission church San Carlos,
  Builded by Carmelo's Bay,
There remains an ivied ruin
  That is crumbling fast away.
In its tower the owls find shelter,
  In its sanctuary grow
Rankest weeds above the earth-mound,
  And the dead find rest below.

Still, by peasants at Carmelo,
  Tales are told and songs are sung
Of Junipero the Padre
  In the sweet Castilian tongue:
Telling how each year he rises
  From his grave the mass to say,
In the midnight, mid the ruins,
  On the eve of Carlos' day.

And they tell when, aged and feeble,
    Feeling that his end was nigh,
To the Mission of San Carlos
    Padre Serra came to die;
And he lay upon a litter
    That Franciscan friars bore,
And he bade them rest a moment
    At the cloister's open door.

Then he gazed upon the landscape
    That in beauty lay unrolled,
And he blessed the land as Francis
    Blessed Asisi's town of old;
And he spoke : "A hundred masses
    I will sing, if still life's guest,
That the blessing I have given
    On the land may ever rest."

Ere a mass was celebrated
    Good Junipero had died,
And they laid him in the chancel,
    On the altar's gospel side.

But each year the Padre rises
　　From his grave the mass to say,
In the midnight, mid the ruins,
　　On the eve of Carlos' day.

Then the sad souls, long years buried,
　　From their lowly graves arise,
And, as if doom's trump had sounded,
　　Each assumes his mortal guise ;
And they come from San Juan's Mission,
　　From St. Francis by the bay,
From the Mission San Diego,
　　And the Mission San José.

With their gaudy painted banners,
　　And their flambeaux burning bright,
In a long procession come they
　　Through the darkness and the night ;
Singing hymns and swinging censers,
　　Dead folks' ghosts—they onward pass
To the ivy-covered ruins,
　　To be present at the mass.

And the grandsire, and the grandame,
 And their children march along,
And they know not one another
 In that weird, unearthly throng.
And the youth and gentle maiden,
 They who loved in days of yore,
Walk together now as strangers,
 For the dead love nevermore.

In the church now all are gathered,
 And not long have they to wait;
From his grave the Padre rises,
 Midnight mass to celebrate.
First he blesses all assembled,
 Soldiers, Indians, acolytes ;
Then he bows before the altar,
 And begins the mystic rites.

When the Padre sings the *sanctus*,
 And the Host is raised on high,
Then the bells up in the belfry,
 Swung by spirits, make reply ;

And the drums roll, and the soldiers
    In the air a volley fire,
While the *salutaris* rises
    Grandly from the phantom choir.

" *Ite, misa est,*" is spoken
    At the dawning of the day,
And the pageant strangely passes
    From the ruins sere and gray;
And Junipero the Padre
    Lying down, resumes his sleep,
And the tar-weeds, rank and noisome,
    O'er his grave luxuriant creep.

And the lights upon the altar
    And the torches cease to burn,
And the vestments and the banners
    Into dust and ashes turn;
And the ghostly congregation
    Cross themselves, and, one by one,
Into thin air swiftly vanish,
    And the midnight mass is done.

WAITING FOR THE GALLEON.

Good Junipero the Padre
    With Portala stood one day
By the church at San Diego,
    Gazing o'er the tranquil bay
To the mystic line where ocean
    And the sky were linked in one,
Waiting for a sign or token
    Of an absent galleon.

This same galleon departed
    For San Blas three months before,
To return with food and raiment,
    For fast dwindling was their store;
And yet, since the time she vanished
    From the dim horizon's line,
To the Mission San Diego
    Came no token or no sign.

Then spoke Governor Portala:
  "Padre Serra, since the day
That the galleon departed
  Full three months have passed away;
Now the only safety left us,
  Since our store is running low,
Is to leave this barren Mission,
  And march back to Mexico."

Serra stood awhile in silence,
  And his eyes welled up with tears;
In that moment seemed to vanish
  All the toil and hope of years.
Then he answered thus : " Portala,
  You may go, but I remain;
For I know that Heaven will bring us
  Back the galleon again.

" But I beg of you, still longer
  Your march southward to delay;
Stay at San Diego's Mission
  Till at least St. Joseph's day."

Then the Governor made answer :
  " As you wish it, be it so;
If she come not on the feast-day,
  I march back to Mexico."

Then the Padre and the soldier
  Stood and watched, day after day,
By the church at San Diego,
  Gazing o'er the tranquil bay—
To the mystic line where ocean
  And the sky were linked in one,
Waiting for a sign or token
  Of the absent galleon.

'Twas at last Saint Joseph's feast-day,
  And Portala, as he passed
From Presidio to Mission,
  To the sea a long look cast;
Cloudless, clear, and calm the sky was,
  And he smiled, as well he might—
For the ocean lay all tranquil,
  And there was no sail in sight.

At the church, the mass is finished,
    Tears and prayers do not avail;
Heaven has sent no sign nor token,
    In the offing is no sail;
And the little congregation
    On their several ways have gone,
And before the humble altar
    Padre Serra kneels alone.

Thus he prays: "Though all desert me
    I will stay, whate'er may come;
Be it fire, or sword, or famine,
    Tears, or pain, or martyrdom.
In my every act, O Father!
    I would seek Thy guidance still.
If I fail to do Thy bidding,
    'Tis I misconstrue Thy will,

" And am like the weary sailor,
    When the landmarks all are hid,
And the lights on shore that guided,
    Night, and fogs, and mists amid,

Seeking still to make the haven,
   And, all anxious though he be
To reach home, and love, and shelter,
   Wanders farther out to sea.

"Let me journey not in darkness,
   Show a light, O Father mine!
Stretch Thy guiding hand still earthward,
   Give my doubting heart a sign;
Grant that prayers, and toil, and watching
   May not all have been in vain;
If it be but for a moment
   Bring the galleon again."

As Junipero the Padre
   By the altar bended low,
Suddenly a cannon thundered
   From the near Presidio;
Then "A sail! a sail!" was echoed
   By the watchers on the shore,
And a ringing cheer of welcome
   Hailed the galleon once more.

From the church-door gazed the Padre,
 And lo! in the noonday sun,
He beheld, on far horizon,
 The long-wished-for galleon;
From her peak the red-cross floating,
 With her colors bright and gay,
And her white sail broadly swelling,
 As if making for the bay.

While the Indians gazed with wonder,
 And the Spaniards cheered or wept,
And the Padre knelt, thanks giving,
 Still the galleon onward kept.
But the mists rose from the ocean,
 While they wept, or prayed, or cheered,
Hiding from their view the vessel,
 So she strangely disappeared.

Then the Padre Serra, rising,
 Pointed to the mystic line,
And addressed the wondering gazers :
 " Children, saw ye not the sign ?

Yet the galleon it was not,
    It was but a thing of air,
Penciled on the sky by angels,
    As an answer to our prayer."

Then he spoke unto Portala :
    " Do you still intend to go
And desert our struggling Mission?"
    And the Governor said, " No ;
Though my troops now all are ready
    For the march, yet I obey
The command sent down from heaven,
  . And here with you I will stay."

Then the Padre and Portala
    Stood and watched, day after day,
By the church at San Diego,
    Gazing o'er the tranquil bay ;
Till the third day had passed over,
    When there suddenly appeared
The good galleon, long wished-for,
    And now straight to land she steered.

Hours and hours her course still holding,
    Scarce a breeze her sail to swell,
From the dawning, through the noon-time,
    Till the shades of evening fell;
Then the *San Antonio*, laden
    With supplies, in safety lay,
By the Mission San Diego,
    Anchored in the tranquil bay.

Then told Don Juan Perez, Captain
    Of the *San Antonio:*
"From the ocean rose this mission
    In the noon three days ago;
Yet, though wind filled up our broad sail,
    When we tried to reach the land
Something seemed to intercept us
    That we could not understand.

"But we steered with broad sail swelling
    For the tranquil bay, when lo!
The adobe white-walled Mission
    And the gray Presidio;

And the soldiers, Spaniards, Indians,
 And the green and pleasant land,
Faded like mirage, or day-dream—
 And we could not understand.

"Then we feared, by fogs surrounded,
 Still to hug a dangerous coast;
So we drifted out to ocean,
 All our course and reckoning lost;
And for three long days we drifted,
 While we thought that nevermore
We should see the white-walled Mission,
 And our loved ones on the shore.

"On the third day passed the fog-mist,
 And the sun gleamed bright and clear,
And the wind filled up our broad sail,
 And we knew no longer fear;
And we floated on a current,
 Swift as swallow in its flight,
Till the Mission San Diego
 Rose again upon our sight."

Tnus the Captain, Don Juan Perez,
    Told about his long delay
While the *San Antonio*, anchored,
    Lay in San Diego Bay,
And said Serra: "God has surely
    Brought this galleon again,
As a sign that at this Mission
    'Tis His will we should remain."

By the Bay of San Diego,
    Still the aged Spaniards tell
How the vessel on the feast-day
    Was shown by a miracle;
How the California missions
    Were preserved by God's command,
And the *San Antonio*, laden
    With supplies came back to land;

How each year, at San Diego,
    As a proof of this true tale,
On the feast-day of Saint Joseph
    There is seen a phantom sail

On the dim line of horizon
   As the sail was seen of old—
But the gossips hint those only
   Who are pure of heart behold.

DISCOVERY OF SAN FRANCISCO BAY.

Good Junipero the Padre
    Slowly read the King's commands,
In relation to the missions
    To be built in heathen lands.
And he said: "The good Saint Francis
    Surely has some little claim,
Yet I find that here no mission
    Is assigned unto his name."

Then the Visitador answered;
    "If the holy Francis care
For a mission to his honor
    Surely he will lead you there;
And it may be by the harbor
    That the Indian legends say
Lies by greenest hills surrounded
    To the north of Monterey."

Spoke Junipero the Padre;
    " It is not for me to tell
Of the truth of Indian legends,
    Yet of this I know full well—
If there be such hidden harbor,
    And our hope and trust we place
In the care of good Saint Francis,
    He will guide us to the place."

Soon, the Governor Portala
    Started northward, on his way
Overland, to rediscover
    The lost port of Monterey.
Since the time within its waters
    Viscaino anchor cast,
It remained unknown to Spaniards,
    Though a century had passed.

On his journey went Portala
    With his band of pioneers,
Padres, Indian guides, and soldiers,
    And a train of muleteers;

And said Serra, as he blessed them,
    As he wished them all Godspeed:
"Trust Saint Francis--he will guide you
    In your direst hour of need."

On his journey went Portala
    Till he reached the crescent bay,
But he dreamed not he was gazing
    On the wished-for Monterey.
So a cross on shore he planted,
    And the ground about he blessed,
And then he and his companions
    Northward went upon their quest.

On his journey went Portala
    And his army northward on,
And methinks I see them marching,
    Or in camp when day was done;
Or at night when stars were twinkling,
    As that travel-weary band
By the log-fire's light would gather,
    Telling of their far-off land.

And they told weird Indian legends,
    Tales of Cortes, too, they told,
And of peaceful reign of Incas,
    And of Montezuma's gold;
And they sang, as weary exiles
    Sing of home and vanished years,
Sweet, heart-treasured songs that always
    Bring the dumb applause of tears.

When the day was sunk in ocean,
    And the land around was dim,
On the tranquil air of midnight
    Rose the sweet Franciscan hymn;
And when bugle told the dawning,
    And the matin prayers were done,
On his journey went Portala
    And his army northward on.

Far away they saw sierras,
    Clothed with an eternal spring,
While at times the mighty ocean
    In their path her spray would fling;

On amid such scenes they journeyed,
   Through the dreary wastes of sand,
Through ravines dark, deep, and narrow,
   And through cañons wild and grand.

And with what a thrill of pleasure,
   All their toils and dangers through,
Gazed they on this scene of beauty
   When it burst upon their view,
As Portala and his army,
   Standing where I stand to-day,
Saw before them spread in beauty
   Green-clad hills and noble bay.

Then the Governor Portala
   Broke the spell of silence thus :
"To this place through Padre Serra
   Hath Saint Francis guided us,
So the bay and all around it
   For the Spanish King I claim,
And forever, in the future,
   Let it bear Saint Francis' name " ·

Thus he spoke—and I am standing
  On the self-same spot to-day,
And my eyes rest on the landscape,
  And the green hills, and the bay,
And upon Saint Francis' city,
  As, with youth and hope elate,
She is gazing toward the ocean,
  Sitting by the Golden Gate.

Needless were such gifts as heaven
  Gave to holy seers of yore,
To foretell the meed of glory,
  Fairest town, for thee in store !
To foretell the seat of empire
  Here will be, nor far the day,
Where Balboa's sea doth mingle
  With the waters of thy bay !

THE HOME ON THE PLAIN.

Bright angels, guarding o'er the land,
 Were looking down from heaven afar;
Each held a lantern in his hand,
 The light of which men call a star.

And o'er the plain, as night came on,
 Two weary pilgrims held their way;
They came from Mission of San Juan,
 And sought the Mission Monterey.

Spoke Padre Serra: "Brother, here
 Must we one night at least remain;
So gratefully and without fear
 Let us repose upon the plain."

As on the ground knelt down the two,
 A light amid the darkness shone;

And suddenly upon their view
    A house appeared, some distance on.

Said Palou : "Surely food and rest
    The Devil brings us now to tempt;
My flesh is weak, and from such test
    I'd rather wish to be exempt."

But vanished soon all fear away,
    For by the door an old man stood,
Who welcomed them and bade them stay
    And share his humble roof and food.

They entered ; everything was neat,
    A lady fair and lovely boy
Received them; 'twas a home complete,
    Where all was love, and peace, and joy.

That night the pilgrims rested there,
    And soon as came the dawn of day,
Thanking their hosts for rest and fare,
    They went rejoicing on their way.

Soon met they with a muleteer,
        Who said: "So far from men's abode
I wonder much to meet ye here;
        How fare ye on this desert road?"

"Some two miles hence last night we staid."·
        Then wondered more the muleteer:
" Some error surely you have made—
        No house for sixty miles is near.

" So if two miles from this last night
        You staid and met with kindly fare,
And slept in peace till morning's light,
        'Twas God who entertained you there."

"Why, still in sight the house must lie,"
        The Padre said; but lo! 'twas gone;
And as they gazed in azure sky,
        The morning star in beauty shone.

Spoke after pause, the Padre thus:
        " Slowly the truth has come to me;

Bright angels ministered to us,
    And very blessed were the three;

"By spirit hands was built that house,
    And the old man whom we saw there
Was Joseph, the good Virgin's spouse,
    And Mary was the lady fair.

"And well I know the youth was he,
    The meek and lowly Nazarene,
Who died for us on Calvary,
    The thief and penitent between."

THE OLD FORTY-NINER.

'Another pioneer is gone."
    The *Alta California* said ;
And still the heedless world wagged on,
    Nor paused when one so great was dead.

At night he sat beside the stove,
    And while he puffed a steady blast,
His wandering memory would rove
    To some strange stories of the past.

And we would gather round to hear
    The old man tell of by-gone days,
Of miner's camp and rugged cheer,
    And early comers' reckless ways.

His great forte was in argument—
    Not that he logic understood,

But facts he could with ease invent;
  Likewise his lungs were very good.

He argued with the greatest zest,
  'Twas difficult to put him out;
And strange to say, he talked the best
  Of what he knew the least about.

When one a stubborn fact would bring,
  He thus would say: "Young friend of mine,
You cannot tell me anything,
  For I've been here since forty-nine."

He told us once of dreadful ride,
  By red men tracked through tule grass;
And how, when all seemed safe, there died,
  By random shot, his Indian lass.

"I raised her up, but she was dead;
  My own dear wife—ah! cruel fates!"
We pitied him, but then he said:
  "My other wife is in the States."

VIRGINIA CITY.

The greatest mining town the world all over,
    Far back as 'fifty-nine its history goes;
A rich lead then did Comstock here discover,
    And from his camp Virginia City rose.

Perched on the steep hill-side, one may well wonder
    What is it keeps the place from tumbling down;
Five thousand men being its foundations under,
    Tearing away all that supports the town.

Thus sometimes earth will open and will swallow
    Some structure, masterpiece of mason's craft,
So rapidly that eye doth vainly follow,
    As it goes thundering down a mining-shaft.

I hold that he, who in the mines doth labor,
    Becomes inhuman in his thirst for gold;

Love, faith, and joy have never more the savor
    For him that they were wont to have of old.

The bed-rock's cold, inhospitable nature
    He doth absorb; it grows of him a part;
Though outwardly a man in form and stature,
    A piece of rock within beats for a heart.

And yet his trade is dangerous and trying;
    The wall caves in, untimed goes off the blast,
Gases explode, and soon "on top" is flying
    The stars and stripes, but half-way up the mast.

The youth and maiden in their moonlight ramble,
    Of Savage, Crown Point, and of Belcher talk;
For Cupid here with silver quartz doth gamble,
    And lovers all in mining-claims have stock.

Yes, each one's hope is upon stocks relying;
    They sweeten or add gall to every cup;
The preacher whispers to the Christian dying:
    "Depart in peace, for stocks are looking up."

That all are bad, you would be wrong in deeming ;
  Some noble hearts doth still Virginia hold,
Like her own quartz, which though rough and un-
    seeming,
  Has in it still veins of the purest gold.

IN ST. MARY'S HOSPITAL.

"Say, Sister Augustine, for you
    The long, long night have watch been keeping,
Did any one this ward pass through,
    And bend o'er me as I lay sleeping?"

Replied the Sister: "No one came
    Into this ward; but you were raving,
And frequently named a mother's name
    While I your fevered brow was laving."

"She came not! then it was a dream,
    And yet I thought o'er me she bended,
And songs of love and home did seem
    Like perfume with her presence blended.

"She told me how she watched and wept,
    While I o'er half the world was roaming:

How by the fire a chair was kept
  Each night, expectant of my coming.

"How the old house seemed lone and drear;
  When all was joy how still she missed me.
I cried : 'Forgive me, mother dear !'
  And bending, on my brow she kissed me.

"'Forgive me that I did resign
  Home with its love and tranquil pleasure,
To toil long years in camp and mine,
  In feverish quest of gold and treasure !'

"Again she kissed my fevered brow,
  The fever with her kiss departed;
You see I have no fever now,
  New life through all my frame has started."

O, mother's love! O, wondrous power !
  Thy memory is balm supplying
To soothe with dreams the latest hour
  Of stranger in a far land dying.

CHEMISE JOE.

Above our heads the noonday sun was standing,
    Blasting the tule with its scorching heat ;
Before us was the little town, Knight's Landing,
    The Sacramento rippling at its feet.

A something seemed to hide at our approaching—
    The driver slacked his speed, and pointing low,
Said : "Yonder, 'mid the underbrush, is crouching
    The wild man of Colusa, 'Chemise Joe.'"

"And who is he?" quoth I.   Dale Houx made answer :
    "You must be strange in these parts not to know—
Why, all the State has heard about that man, sir;
    They call him 'Chaparral' or 'Chemise Joe.'

"His only roof is the broad arch of heaven ;
    He never wearies of his solitude,

And only when by pangs of hunger driven
    He seeks some shepherd's hut, and begs for food."

I asked: "Why shuns he thus man's happy dwelling
    To live in misery and care alone?"
Dale Houx replied: "Indeed, there is no telling—
    Perhaps he has some reason of his own."

Said I: "Perhaps he seeks, by prayer and fasting,
    The expiation of unshriven sins."
The driver spoke, on me a keen eye casting:
    "It may have been, sir, that his wife had twins."

Then I: "Perhaps in rage he struck a brother,
    Or missed a fortune by some legal flaw,
Or in his early childhood lost a mother."
    Said Houx: "Perhaps he found a mother-in-law."

"Perhaps his heart, with some sweet face delighted,
    Its tendrils tangled amid golden locks,
To find at last its love was not requited."
    Said Houx: "Perhaps he busted up in stocks."

Said I : "Perhaps the friendship tnat he trusted
 When came misfortune's hour was found to fail."
Said Houx: "It may have been he up and dusted,
 Leaving behind his bondsmen for his bail."

"Perhaps," said I, "unto the god Apollo
 He tunes his lyre—one of the poet craft."
Said Houx: "It somehow seems to me to follow
 A poet always is a little daft."

Perceiving that the driver only needed
 A word of mine to give his fancy play,
I did not make reply, so we proceeded
 In silence on our long and sultry way.

And when we reached the town, our journey's ending,
 Said I : "You must be thirsty—let us drink."
The driver, from his seat with speed descending,
 Grasping my hand, and with a merry wink,

Made answer thus : "Why, you are talking reason.
 I do not drink; but, seeing it is you,
And irrigation's right in this dry season,
 Well, stranger, now I don't mind if I do."

CACHEVILLE.

Far in the Sacramento Valley, down
    Amid the lands in tule, is Cacheville;
But did they call it Chills-and Fever Town,
    I think 'twere better still.

And for the stream, so sickly and so small,
    That flows near by, apt title did they seek,
It, for variety's sake, they might call
    By name of Dead-Man's Creek.

No season respite here for plague doth bring—
    The very cats and dogs with ague die,
And birds that o'er the town their passage wing
    Go trembling through the sky.

Through its malarious streets its people wend,
    With fever flushed, or shivering with the chills,

And as one offers snuff unto a friend
    They offer ague pills.

Or silently they sit, with care cast down,
    Beside the fire, who once were glad and brave,
For every hearthstone in this wretched town
    Is tomb above a grave.

There is a school-house; but the merry sound
    Of play and laughter it can little know,
For close beside it is the burial-ground,
    And there the children go.

This grave-yard is much larger than the town,
    And strangers smile to read upon the stones
The name significant of Arsenic Brown,
    Or that of Quinine Jones.

I think the trade of coffin-maker here,
    Or that of undertaker, well must pay–
There is a babe born about once a year,
    A man dies every day.

If it should ever chance that you be down,
　My friend, close by the place of which I speak,
Then do not visit Chills-and-Fever Town,
　And shun the Dead-Man's Creek.

OFF SANTA BARBARA.

Off Santa Barbara at break of day
      Our steamer lay,
While I more southward, for San Pedro bound,
      Was sleeping sound,
Unconscious that the scene more lovely seemed
Than fairest fancy ever poet dreamed.

A little bright-eyed child, with golden hair,
      Ah, passing fair!
Into my state-room almost noiseless crept,
      While still I slept,
And coming to my bed, no word she spoke,
But bending downward kissed me and I woke.

"Why, what can be the matter now?" I said.
      With downcast head
She tried to speak, but knew not what to say,
      Then rushed away;

I came on deck, but she had gone on shore,
And so her pretty face I saw no more.

Crowned with green hills, an almost Aiden land
　　　　Lay on one hand,
While on the other, in immensity,
　　　　Balboa's sea
Was stretching far as eye could reach away,
With gulls upon its throbbing breast at play.

The Mission church do I remember still
　　　　Upon the hill;
And fancy, while the bells sung matin chimes
　　　　Strayed to old times,
Until I seemed to hear good Serra say:
"Oh, gentiles, come to holy church and pray."

The air was fragrant with the rich perfume
　　　　Of orange bloom,
The giant trees with fruit were laden down,
　　　　Quaint looked the town,

Whose folk, with joy's o'erflowing measure blest,
Could each beneath his vine and fig-tree rest.

O, Santa Barbara, the beautiful!
   Though time may dull
The glowing pictures that remain of thee
   In memory,
Still in my heart her little face I keep,
As, o'er me bent, she kissed me from my sleep.

JUNIPERO SERRA.

Within the ruined church at Carmel's bay,
    Beside the altar, with rank weeds o'ergrown,
    There is a grave unmarked with slab or stone,
Where lies one who, lost sight of in our day,
Yet bides his time; and when have passed away
    Our would-be heroes, he will then be known,
    And glory's heritage at last will own,
His title to which no one will gainsay.
When life was nearing to an end, 'twas here,
    Seeking repose, the Padre Serra came;
Of our fair land he was the pioneer:
    And if the good alone were known to fame,
Within our hearts his memory would be dear,
    And on our lips a household word his name.

MINING.

The shaft some thousand fathoms I descended,
    To where stout miners worked 'mid endless night,
    The walls reflected back my taper's light
As through these catacombs of gold I wended,
I saw the rocks from where God placed them rended
    By patient stroke of pick and muscle's might,
    And then I saw the metal fair and bright
Cleared of the dross with which 'twas whilom blended.
I said, while watching them the quartz refine,
    The poet with these toilers is akin ;
    Although a different meed he seeks to win,
Yet he, instructed by a power divine,
    Selects from thoughts ignoble, mean, and poor,
    The golden ones that ever must endure.

SAN FRANCISCO.

Though night has come upon the hills, I stay,
   And my eyes, resting in their downward glances,
   Fall on the fair young city of Saint Francis—
The dim Sierra fading fast away,
The fleet of anchored ships, the noble bay
   Upon whose rippling waves the moonlight dances,
   And Golden Gate through which the fog advances
That will soon hide the scene with cowl of gray.
O City watching by Balboa's sea !
   Thine is the future, and sure faith I hold
   When greed of gain and lawlessness are past,
Thou wilt have brighter days, for thou wilt be
   A home of science, art, and song at last,
   As Rome and Athens were in days of old.

THE OLD SAD STRAIN.

When the weary, home-bound sailor
　　Is clinging aloft to the shroud,
He heeds not the rising gale or
　　The breakers roaring loud;
For his thoughts their flight go winging
　　Across the storm-tossed main,　　.
And he hears sweet voices singing
　　In his home the old sad strain.

And when the exiles assemble
　　At night round the roaring blaze,
The voices grow husky and tremble
　　That tell of the vanished days;
And while they speak, there doth glisten
　　In each one's eye a tear,
Not alone to the tales they listen,
　　For the old sad strain they hear.

Beside the fire I am staying,
    Though the night be on the wane,
For spirit hands are playing
    In my heart the old sad strain.
Though sad it is, yet such is
    The sweetness of every note,
As if by angels' touches
    The chords of life were smote.

The strain shall never be gayer,
    But always with sadness be blent,
Till the time the Master-player
    Shall take up the instrument;
And at the touch of his fingers
    A happier strain will start,
Than the old sad one that lingers
    Within this weary heart.

THE PAWNBROKER'S SHOP.

In my walks through the city I frequently stop
To examine the wares in the pawnbroker's shop,
For each article here has a story to tell
Unto all who interpret its voicelessness well.
These were emblems of friendship and truth long ago,
But their presence here sorrow and misery show,
For they tell of estrangements and fond ones grown
      cold—
Once the pledges of love, now the pledges of gold.

Let us enter awhile: lady fair, do not fear,
The great ones of earth in their time have been here;
Here have come youth and maid, and the old and the
      gray;
Here the peer and the pauper have elbowed their way;
The exchequers of kings from such shops have been
      drawn,
And the jewels of queens have been given in pawn.

Then enter, and if for awhile you will stop,
I will tell of the wares in the pawnbroker's shop.

Here's a little gold cross; 'twas a tremulous hand
Placed it round her boy's neck ere he left the old land.
Though that good mother prayed 'twould a talisman
      be
To the youth in his new home beyond the great sea.
Though he clung to it fondly for many a year,
For a dollar or two he at last sold it here;
Yet the treasures of earth were the veriest dross
When compared to the value he placed on this cross.

Here's a locket of hair, once a bright sunny curl,
It was shorn from her locks by a beautiful girl,
And she gave it to him whom as life she held dear,
While he whispered a tale of fond love in her ear;
Her life's blood that girl would have given to prove
The strength, and devotion, and depth of her love.
Was love true to the last, till the warm heart grew cold,
Or like this, its dear gift, was it bartered for gold?

Here's a gold wedding-ring; many years must have
    gone   .
Since two knelt in the church, and with this were made
    one.
O, who would not envy the bride in that hour,
With everything earth could bestow for a dower!
As the groom on her fair finger placed this gold ring,
Ah, little he thought time such changes could bring
As that here she should come, youth and beauty all
    fled,
And her wedding-ring pawn to get money for bread.

But enough I have sung, and though sad be my lay,
Yet a much sadder theme you may find any day,
When poverty made them these love-tokens sell;
What matter if honor were not sold as well!
If you go through the town you will daily behold
Both manhood and maidenhood bartered for gold,
And these, till time's ending, forever will stop
Unredeemed, if once brought to the pawnbroker's
    shop.

A SONG IN THE PLAY.

It was a gala-night in truth,
    The master's play was on:
O'er beauty, wealth, and wit, and youth,
    A brilliant halo shone.

A very queen the chief part played,
    With such a studied grace,
The meaning of each word was weighed
    Each tone, and glance of face.

A song 's sung by the heroine,
    But as this tragic dame
Sung not, to take her place, a thin
    And frightened girl there came.

A girl in faded muslin dress
    Stood scared and trembling there,

Without an ornament, unless
    A flower twined in her hair;

While fearful that the song might fail,
    There stood revealed to all,
Beside the wing, a mother pale,
    With her daughter's tattered shawl.

The poor girl sang quite tenderly—
    Hers was no trick of art,
Its soft sweet tones appeared to be
    Up-welling from the heart.

A simple song, and yet it seemed
    The hearts of all to stir,
And rough men hid their eyes and dreamed
    Of happy times that were.

Ah, yes! and when the song was done,
    Sobs mingled with their cheers;
The sweetest singer is the one
    That moves us most to tears.

She bowed, and to her cheek there came
    A blush that made her fair—
A bright, warm blush, that put to shame
    The rouge and powder there.

And sweeter than before she sung
    The same sad, simple lay;
While with applause the whole house rung,
    The poor girl swooned away.

Not over-pleased the tragic queen
    Again came on the stage;
Her studied walk and somber mien
    Did now small thought engage;

Or, seemed but clearer to recall
    To that excited throng
The mother with the tattered shawl,
    The poor girl's touching song.

THE SUPPLIANT.

Four spirits, late of earth, once stood beside
The gate of Paradise and entrance sought:
To them the Guardian Angel thus replied:
"None enter here save those who good have wrought."

Then each of them in turn his merits said:
The first: "I stood before the grave of Time,
And, like a Savior, cited forth the dead
To rise and live forever in my rhyme."

Another, thus: "A sculptor I, and such
The beauty was that I to stone did give,
My statues wanted but a single touch
Of God's right hand to make them breathe and live."

The third: "I rivaled nature with my dyes;
And to the sad earth, in its darkest hours,

My pencil brought again the summer skies,
The laughing brooks, the verdure and the flowers."

They entered; but without still lingered one,
To whom thus spoke the Angel: "We would know
Upon the earth what good deeds you have done.".
"Alas!" he answered, "I have none to show.

"A Suppliant am I for entrance here;
But when in Mercy's God my hope I place,
Like dead men's ghosts the sins of many a year
Rise up in mockery before my face."

The Angel: "Go! there is no room for thee."
And as the Suppliant turned, in tears, away,
The spirits, with one voice, imploringly
Cried unto him: "Stay with us, brother, stay."

And then the spirits told how he had done
Kind deeds on earth, and one spoke thus: "I fear
If he unworthy be, no single one
Of us is worthy of remaining here."

They told: "I hungered, and he gave me meat;"
" His draught of water did my thirst allay;"
" I passed his happy home with weary feet,
  And he did follow me and bid me stay;"

" Ill-clad was I; he gave me clothes to wear;"
" In lazar-house, when every friend did flee,
  He nursed me through a loathsome sickness there;"
" I was in prison and he came to me."

The Angel spoke: " There is no room for thee."
  Then spirit fairer than the rest, did say:
" Good Angel, out of charity to me,
  Ah, do not turn yon Suppliant away;

" But rather bid him stay, and I will give
  My place to him; of right it is his own,
  And I will go back to the earth and live
  Far from my Maker's face and His bright throne."

To whom the Angel: " Sister, is the stain
  Of earthly love upon thy spirit still,

That thou wouldst go back to the world again
That he who loved thee might thy place here fill?"

" I would not ask for him, were he the one—
　Repentant tears did all such love erase ;
　But every earthly feeling is not gone,
　Still in my heart has gratitude a place ;

" And he whom thou wouldst from thy bright gate
　　　spurn,
　Found me, one time, an outcast on the town ;
　He raised me up to God.　'Tis now my turn,
　And I will give to him my glory crown."

　Back of itself, upon its hinges swung
　The gate of pearl, e'en as the words were said,
　And while in joy the choir of spirits sung,
　Within the walls the Suppliant was led.

DOWN THE LANE.

The year was drawing to its end,
    The dusk was mingling with the day,
As I in dreamy mood did wend
    Adown the lane my lonely way.

Like trellis-work across the sky,
    From either side rose arching trees,
Whose boughs were swaying fitfully,
    Whose leaves were dangling in the breeze,

Or as they fell upon the ground
    Were eddied into many a heap,
Which rustling winds with mournful sound
    Did thinly o'er my pathway sweep.

And as I went a drizzling rain,
    Across my face came slanting down,

While passed me many a loaded wain
  And peasant hastening to the town.

The dreariness that round me lay,
  The withered leaf tossed in the wind,
The drip that plashed the miry way,
  Seemed kindred all unto my mind.

But then I thought me : " This decay
  The germ doth bear of future bloom,
Like those few grains of wheat that lay
  In hand of death in Egypt's tomb.

" For though in rot resolves the leaf,
  The parching clay 'twill fertilize,
And from it soon the harvest sheaf
  And fragrant blossoms will arise.

" Ay, ay," methought, " there draweth nigh
  A merry time of bloom again,
Of beauteous flowers, of tranquil sky,
  And unto me doth hope remain

"That He who summer sun doth bring
    Who decks in grandeur every tree,
  Who bids again the wild bird sing,
    Has happy days in store for me."

RECESS.

The little folks have now recess,
    In merry groups they play.
Once I, whom sorrows now oppress,
    Was light of heart as they,
As gay was I in years gone by,
    Though very sad to-day.

I close the tome of ancient lore
    And rest it on my knee;
Sweet voices and gay laughter more
    Of pleasure bring to me;
To me they bring youth's golden spring
    And joys that used to be.

Life's summer-time is on the wane,
    Its fire is burning low;
Winds sweep the hearth, and lo! again
    The dying embers glow.

They glow, they blaze, and bygone days
    Come back from long ago.

The weary book aside I fling,
    I stretch my arms apart,
And youth and love on spirit wing
    Come fluttering to my heart.
Ah, nestle there, ye happy pair,
    And nevermore depart!

CHILDREN'S HYMN.

Our hymn in praise of One shall be
    Who to the parents said,
" Let little ones come unto me,
    Of such my home is made;"
Who, when we sleep, keeps watching o'er,
    And brings such happy dreams,
That earthly cares annoy no more,
    And heaven around us seems.

Who knows e'en our most trivial need,
    Who knows the thought untold,
And who will every kindly deed
    Repay a thousand-fold.
Ah! let us, then, his praises sing,
    And humbly ask that he,
Through storm and night our barks may bring
    Unto the tranquil sea.

When all around is drear and dim,
    And we have gone astray,
If we but lift our hands to him,
    He guides us on our way.
Ah ! let us then our voices raise,
    And tell him of our love,
And we will ever sing his praise
    In happiness above.

CHINAMPHAS.

It cometh from the mountain steeps
    Afar off where the waters rise,
And by the still lagoon it creeps,
    And down the rapid swiftly flies.

It is a fair and flower-clad isle
    That seems as if by some device
Its moorings to have slipped awhile
    And drifted down from Paradise.

Trees round it, tall and beautiful,
    Shelter it from the burning noon;
And dark-faced men the long oars pull,
    And sing low-toned some love-born tune.

It brings down flowers to deck the shrine,
    Or o'er the bride's brow to be wove,

Or for the stricken heart to twine
  Around the tomb of buried love.

So unto me, aye, even while
  The current of my life shall flow,
Will be a fair and flower-clad isle, ·
  Like those fair isles of Mexico!

And still mid many a shifting scene,
  Where'er my wandering way be cast,
That little isle will still be green
  With pleasant memories of the past.

THE MOTHER'S PRAYER.

A winter's night—the wind was blowing wild
    Around a home where want and sorrow dwelt,
And by the bedside of a dying child
    In tears and prayers a widowed mother knelt.

And lo! an angel bright stood by her side,
    To whom the mother: "Wherefore do you
      come?"
And tenderly the shining one replied:
  "To take your darling to a happier home."

The mother spoke: "'Tis cruel and unkind
    To take my child and let me linger still."
The angel: "Mother, if you were not blind,
    You would bow down in reverence to His will."

The mother said, "Much sorrow I have seen;
    Filled to the brim with care and misery

My cup of life for many years has been;
    Then do not take my only joy from me."

The angel answered : " If a mother's tears
    Might change the ruling of the God above,
And if your son might live to manhood's years,
    No blessing, but a curse, the change would
        prove."

" I care not what his lot in life may be,"
    The mother sobbed, "but leave my little dear."
" You care not," said the angel; " list to me,
    And from his life one passage you will hear:

" Your son will woo a maiden fair and good,
    And win her from her home and country life,
And she will barter truth and maidenhood
    To be to him his everything but wife.

" And he will tire of the poor girl at last,
    And on a night like this, of storm and sleet,
With baby in her arms she shall be cast
    Out of her home to perish in the street."

The mother rose.   " My prayer I do recall.
　　Take him.   A single tear I will not shed.
If by his living one poor soul might fall,
　　I would a thousand times that he were dead."

The angel spoke: " A mother's love is true.
　　I take your little one, but he will wait,
Sinless and beautiful, to welcome you,
　　When life is o'er, beside the jasper gate."

And saying this, he vanished from the place,
　　And as the mother knelt beside the bed,
She kissed her little infant's pallid face,
　　And spoke: " I thank Thee, God, that he is
　　　dead."

THE MASTERPIECE OF BROTHER FELIX.

Two monks were in a cell at close of day—
    A cell that, too, the artist's craft portrayed.
Dying upon a bed the younger lay,
    The older one beside him knelt and prayed.

The older spoke: "Your end is very near—
    To see another day you cannot live;
So banish thought of earth, my brother dear,
    And to your soul alone all thought now give."

"Nay, Francis," said the other, "speak not so;
    I cannot die, my life-work incomplete.
Were that but finished, I would willing go—
    Then death would be a messenger most sweet."

Then Francis spoke: "The world counts the success,
    But God will judge by what you have essayed;

And though you fail, He will not deem the less
    The efforts and the struggles you have made.

" The painter's earthly triumph is but brief—
    A passion-flower is fame, that soon decays;
There is a poison in the laurel leaf,
    While green the wreath of heaven keeps always."

And Felix answered: " Brother Francis, so
    You dream I hanker after earthly fame.
I sought for it one time—'twas long ago—
    But now a holier, better meed I claim ;

" And if grim Death were standing by the gate,
    A messenger who brought the final call,
I tell you, brother, that he still should wait
    Till I had done yon picture on the wall.

" Nay, more—were I beside the golden throne,
    I would bend down at the Almighty's feet,
And beg with tears: ' My life-work is not done—
    Let me return until it be complete.'

" Of praying, therefore, speak not now to me—
  Or, if you pray, pray that I still may live
Until my painting all completed be,
  That I to coming time the work may give."

" God give you grace, my brother," Francis said,
  " Your heart submissive to His will to keep."
And then he turned away, and silent prayed ;
  But soon, o'ercome with watching, fell asleep.

Then from his bed to rise up Felix tried,
  But with the effort, faint and weak, fell back;
Then, clasping hands imploringly, he cried :
  " O God of heaven, one little hour I lack

" To work again upon my masterpiece,
  Till I the face divine have painted there;
I care not then how soon my life may cease.
  Kind God, one hour unto Thy servant spare !

" But death creeps fast; too weak is now my hand
  To picture true the thought that fills my brain.

Send down an angel from the spirit-land,
    That I may not have dreamed such dream in
        vain!"

The cell door opened as he ceased to speak;
    A young man entered—tall he was and fair,
The glow of youth was mantled on his cheek,
    His eyes were blue, and golden was his hair.

"Why come you?" Felix questioned, "and your
    name?"
    The youth made answer: "I am Angelo,
Who hearing of the Brother Felix's fame,
    Have come that I his wondrous art might know."

Then Felix spoke: "I am the man you seek;
    But I am dying, and have not the power
To teach you aught. My heart and hand are weak,
    But you may aid me in this final hour.

"Take yonder painting—set it on the stand
    Here at my bedside, full within my view—

Palette and pencils all are here at hand;
    Then paint, good youth, as I desire you to.

"'Tis all complete except the Savior's face,
    And that upon the canvas faintly lined,
But still so clear that you may plainly trace
    The features fair and God-like, you will find.

"The face is somewhat of a Jewish cast—
    I sketched it from a beggar in the street.
Ah, little dreamed I then, a few weeks past,
    Another hand my painting would complete!"

Then spoke the youth : "A spirit sure has brought
    Me to your cell, to be, as 'twere, a hand
Acting responsive to your every thought—
    Your faintest wish shall be as a command.

"Speak, and I paint!" The dying Felix spoke
    A few words now and then—no need of much;
The canvas into life and beauty woke
    Beneath the magic of the artist's touch.

The youth at last his pencil laid aside,
    And spoke: "O master mine, your work is
        done;
Can I assist you more?" The monk replied,
  "Go on your way and leave me here alone."

The youth departed, and then Felix prayed:
  "I thank thee, God, and death is now most sweet,
Since Thou its shaft a little while hast staid
    Until my masterpiece is all complete."

Francis was woke up by the matin bell;
    He rose, and lo! the light of early day
Upon the painting of the Savior fell
    That on the easel all completed lay.

In silence Francis by the painting stood;
    The features gleamed as with a love divine,
From hands and feet transpierced gushed forth the
        blood,
  'Twas perfect and complete in every line.

" In truth," then Francis spoke, " no mortal hand
    Has limned the rapturous beauty of that face.
Heaven surely heard his supplication, and
    An angel must have visited the place."

To Felix turning : " Yes, the laurel crown
    Is yours, for you have reached art's proudest
      goal."
Then, bursting into tears, he knelt him down ;
    " May God have mercy on the passing soul !"

IN WAR TIME.

On one side of the plain our army lay,
    Their log-fires brightening as the gloom de-
        scended,
While on the other side, a mile away
    The rebel camp into the night extended.

Rough-bearded heroes of a hundred frays
    Were listening to a song a youth was singing ;
With wistful eyes they watched the leaping blaze,
    Dreaming of scenes that song to them was bring-
        ing.

" Kathleen Mavourneen " 'twas, a song of tears ;
    A song by lovers sung about to sever ;
And sadly thus went the refrain : " For years
    May be we part, and may be 'tis forever."

The sweet words seemed to never weary those
  . Who round the fire in pictured groups were seated,
And many times 'twas sung, and at each close
  The sad refrain was o'er and o'er repeated.

To near, then distant fires, it passed along,
  Until at last, sad, solemn, and sonorous,
From every camp-fire came that sweet love-song,
  And the whole Union Army sang the chorus.

The camp was silent now the song was o'er,
  But all the soldiers stood in wonder, noting
The self-same song that unto them once more
  Upon the calm and still night air came floating,

As if the angels bending from above—
  Upon the memories of earth still dwelling—
Had listening been, and now that song of love
  Unto their God in Paradise were telling!

A moment thus the soldiers may have thought,
  Then whence it came they found with tears up
    springing;

The far-off Rebel troops the song had caught,
    And in their camp the tender words were singing.

Our troops now sang, nor did the Rebels cease;
    In unison the thousand voices blended
Of hostile camps, and to the God of Peace
    That song of love upon the night ascended.

THE MIRAGE.

An Arab, thinking that his death was nigh,
    Sank down beside his camel on the sand,
    When cleared away the mist-cloud, and a land
Of beauty loomed upon his wondering eye—
Green palms their frondage rearing broad and high,
    The ground beneath them with cool breezes fanned,
    While fragrant flowers were seen on every hand,
And birds of song soared in the tranquil sky.
But when to reach that land he did essay
    It faded like dream-picture, and before
Him stretched the desert.   Thus, when by life's way
    We sink, Hope limns bright views of scenes in
        store ;
But when we almost grasp them they decay,
    And Hope her glowing pencil plies no more.

THE POET.

The poet, weary of his task one night,
    Tore up what he had writ and cast aside
    His pen.   Then bending in despair he cried:
"My hope of fame is past—no more I write."
When in a vision came unto his sight
    The jasper gate, and it was open wide;
    And lo! he heard the angel choir inside,
And spoke to him a spirit fair and bright:
    "Oh, treasure in your heart of hearts the strain,
    And when the time is ripe sing it again
Unto the listening world, and you thereby
    Will win the poet's meed—a laurel crown,
    A people's love, and very great renown,
And, when you die, a deathless memory."

DUTY.

A monk, while praying by the early light,
 The holy Nazarene of Calvary saw,
 And bending down in reverence and awe
Gave thanks that to him came so fair a sight.
But even as he spoke he heard the bell,
 Rung by some carl or beggar who did wait
 To gain admittance by the wayside gate ;
And so he rose and straightway left his cell.
And when by night he came some rest to gain
 The Blessed Visitant was still his guest,
 Who thus in loving words the monk addressed :
" You have done well; but if you did remain
 When bidden hence, I should have left the place,
 And you would never more have seen my face."

www.ingramcontent.com/pod-product-compliance
Lightning Source LLC
Chambersburg PA
CBHW022013050726
47499CB00007BA/2567